THIS

MOTORHC ___

ROAD TRIP

TRAVEL JOURNAL

BELONGS TO

NAME ....

EMAIL ....

MOBILE ....

BLOG ....

PLEASE RETURN IF FOUND

MOTORHOME
ROAD TRIP TRAVEL JOURNAL

DATE .... MILEAGE START ....

START TIME .... MILEAGE END ....

ARRIVAL TIME .... MILEAGE TOTAL ....

CAMPSITE NAME ....

ADDRESS 1 ....

ADDRESS 2 ....

POST CODE .... GPS ....

E MAIL .... PHONE ....

WEBSITE WWW..

MY RATING ☆ ☆ ☆ ☆ ☆ NUMBER OF NIGHTS HERE ......

WEATHER .... TEMPERATURE ....

WILDCAMPING LOCATION NOTES

....
....
....
....
.... GPS ....

DAILY COSTS		TODAY'S HIGHLIGHTS
SITE FEES	£	....
FUEL	£	....
PROPANE	£	....
TOLLS	£	....
GROCERIES	£	....
DINING OUT	£	....
ENTERTAINMENT	£	....
OTHER COSTS	£	....

TO DO TOMORROW

....

....

....

....

NOTES

....

....

....

....

....

....

....

....

SKETCH / KEEPSAKE / PHOTOGRAPH

MOTORHOME
ROAD TRIP TRAVEL JOURNAL

DATE .... MILEAGE START ....

START TIME .... MILEAGE END ....

ARRIVAL TIME .... MILEAGE TOTAL ....

CAMPSITE NAME ....

ADDRESS 1 ....

ADDRESS 2 ....

POST CODE .... GPS ....

E MAIL .... PHONE ....

WEBSITE WWW..

MY RATING ☆ ☆ ☆ ☆ ☆ NUMBER OF NIGHTS HERE ......

WEATHER .... TEMPERATURE ....

WILDCAMPING LOCATION NOTES

....
....
....
....
.... GPS ....

DAILY COSTS		TODAY'S HIGHLIGHTS
SITE FEES	£	....
FUEL	£	....
PROPANE	£	....
TOLLS	£	....
GROCERIES	£	....
DINING OUT	£	....
ENTERTAINMENT	£	....
OTHER COSTS	£	....

TO DO TOMORROW

....
....
....
....

NOTES

....

....

....

....

....

....

....

....

SKETCH / KEEPSAKE / PHOTOGRAPH

MOTORHOME
ROAD TRIP TRAVEL JOURNAL

DATE .... MILEAGE START ....

START TIME .... MILEAGE END ....

ARRIVAL TIME .... MILEAGE TOTAL ....

CAMPSITE NAME ....

ADDRESS 1 ....

ADDRESS 2 ....

POST CODE .... GPS ....

E MAIL .... PHONE ....

WEBSITE WWW..

MY RATING ☆ ☆ ☆ ☆ ☆ NUMBER OF NIGHTS HERE ......

WEATHER .... TEMPERATURE ....

WILDCAMPING LOCATION NOTES

....
....
....
....
.... GPS ....

DAILY COSTS		TODAY'S HIGHLIGHTS
SITE FEES	£	....
FUEL	£	....
PROPANE	£	....
TOLLS	£	....
GROCERIES	£	....
DINING OUT	£	....
ENTERTAINMENT	£	....
OTHER COSTS	£	....

TO DO TOMORROW

....

....

....

....

NOTES

....

....

....

....

....

....

....

....

SKETCH / KEEPSAKE / PHOTOGRAPH

MOTORHOME
ROAD TRIP TRAVEL JOURNAL

DATE .... MILEAGE START ....

START TIME .... MILEAGE END ....

ARRIVAL TIME .... MILEAGE TOTAL ....

CAMPSITE NAME ....

ADDRESS 1 ....

ADDRESS 2 ....

POST CODE .... GPS ....

E MAIL .... PHONE ....

WEBSITE WWW..

MY RATING ☆ ☆ ☆ ☆ ☆ NUMBER OF NIGHTS HERE ......

WEATHER .... TEMPERATURE ....

WILDCAMPING LOCATION NOTES

....
....
....
....
.... GPS ....

DAILY COSTS		TODAY'S HIGHLIGHTS
SITE FEES	£	....
FUEL	£	....
PROPANE	£	....
TOLLS	£	....
GROCERIES	£	....
DINING OUT	£	....
ENTERTAINMENT	£	....
OTHER COSTS	£	....

TO DO TOMORROW

....

....

....

....

NOTES

....

....

....

....

....

....

....

....

SKETCH / KEEPSAKE / PHOTOGRAPH

MOTORHOME
ROAD TRIP TRAVEL JOURNAL

DATE .... MILEAGE START ....

START TIME .... MILEAGE END ....

ARRIVAL TIME .... MILEAGE TOTAL ....

CAMPSITE NAME ....

ADDRESS 1 ....

ADDRESS 2 ....

POST CODE .... GPS ....

E MAIL .... PHONE ....

WEBSITE WWW..

MY RATING ☆ ☆ ☆ ☆ ☆ NUMBER OF NIGHTS HERE ......

WEATHER .... TEMPERATURE ....

WILDCAMPING LOCATION NOTES

....
....
....
....
.... GPS ....

DAILY COSTS	TODAY'S HIGHLIGHTS
SITE FEES £	....
FUEL £	....
PROPANE £	....
TOLLS £	....
GROCERIES £	....
DINING OUT £	....
ENTERTAINMENT £	....
OTHER COSTS £	....

TO DO TOMORROW

....
....
....
....

NOTES

....

....

....

....

....

....

....

....

SKETCH / KEEPSAKE / PHOTOGRAPH

MOTORHOME
ROAD TRIP TRAVEL JOURNAL

DATE .... MILEAGE START ....

START TIME .... MILEAGE END ....

ARRIVAL TIME .... MILEAGE TOTAL ....

CAMPSITE NAME ....

ADDRESS 1 ....

ADDRESS 2 ....

POST CODE .... GPS ....

E MAIL .... PHONE ....

WEBSITE WWW...

MY RATING ☆ ☆ ☆ ☆ ☆ NUMBER OF NIGHTS HERE ......

WEATHER .... TEMPERATURE ....

WILDCAMPING LOCATION NOTES

....

....

....

....

.... GPS ....

DAILY COSTS	TODAY'S HIGHLIGHTS
SITE FEES £	....
FUEL £	....
PROPANE £	....
TOLLS £	....
GROCERIES £	....
DINING OUT £	....
ENTERTAINMENT £	....
OTHER COSTS £	....

TO DO TOMORROW

....

....

....

....

NOTES

....

....

....

....

....

....

....

SKETCH / KEEPSAKE / PHOTOGRAPH

MOTORHOME
ROAD TRIP TRAVEL JOURNAL

DATE .... MILEAGE START ....

START TIME .... MILEAGE END ....

ARRIVAL TIME .... MILEAGE TOTAL ....

CAMPSITE NAME ....

ADDRESS 1 ....

ADDRESS 2 ....

POST CODE .... GPS ....

E MAIL .... PHONE ....

WEBSITE WWW...

MY RATING ☆ ☆ ☆ ☆ ☆ NUMBER OF NIGHTS HERE ......

WEATHER .... TEMPERATURE ....

WILDCAMPING LOCATION NOTES

....
....
....
....
.... GPS ....

DAILY COSTS	TODAY'S HIGHLIGHTS
SITE FEES £	....
FUEL £	....
PROPANE £	....
TOLLS £	....
GROCERIES £	....
DINING OUT £	....
ENTERTAINMENT £	....
OTHER COSTS £	....

TO DO TOMORROW

....

....

....

....

NOTES

....

....

....

....

....

....

....

....

SKETCH / KEEPSAKE / PHOTOGRAPH

MOTORHOME
ROAD TRIP TRAVEL JOURNAL

DATE .... MILEAGE START ....

START TIME .... MILEAGE END ....

ARRIVAL TIME .... MILEAGE TOTAL ....

CAMPSITE NAME ....

ADDRESS 1 ....

ADDRESS 2 ....

POST CODE .... GPS ....

E MAIL .... PHONE ....

WEBSITE WWW...

MY RATING ☆ ☆ ☆ ☆ ☆ NUMBER OF NIGHTS HERE ......

WEATHER .... TEMPERATURE ....

WILDCAMPING LOCATION NOTES

....
....
....
.... GPS ....

DAILY COSTS		TODAY'S HIGHLIGHTS
SITE FEES	£	....
FUEL	£	....
PROPANE	£	....
TOLLS	£	....
GROCERIES	£	....
DINING OUT	£	....
ENTERTAINMENT	£	....
OTHER COSTS	£	....

TO DO TOMORROW

....
....
....
....

NOTES

....

....

....

....

....

....

....

....

SKETCH / KEEPSAKE / PHOTOGRAPH

MOTORHOME
ROAD TRIP TRAVEL JOURNAL

DATE .... MILEAGE START ....

START TIME .... MILEAGE END ....

ARRIVAL TIME .... MILEAGE TOTAL ....

CAMPSITE NAME ....

ADDRESS I ....

ADDRESS 2 ....

POST CODE .... GPS ....

E MAIL .... PHONE ....

WEBSITE WWW...

MY RATING ☆ ☆ ☆ ☆ ☆ NUMBER OF NIGHTS HERE ......

WEATHER .... TEMPERATURE ....

WILDCAMPING LOCATION NOTES

....
....
....
....
.... GPS ....

DAILY COSTS	TODAY'S HIGHLIGHTS
SITE FEES £	....
FUEL £	....
PROPANE £	....
TOLLS £	....
GROCERIES £	....
DINING OUT £	....
ENTERTAINMENT £	....
OTHER COSTS £	....

TO DO TOMORROW

....

....

....

....

NOTES

....

....

....

....

....

....

....

SKETCH / KEEPSAKE / PHOTOGRAPH

MOTORHOME
ROAD TRIP TRAVEL JOURNAL

DATE .... MILEAGE START ....

START TIME .... MILEAGE END ....

ARRIVAL TIME .... MILEAGE TOTAL ....

CAMPSITE NAME ....

ADDRESS 1 ....

ADDRESS 2 ....

POST CODE .... GPS ....

E MAIL .... PHONE ....

WEBSITE WWW..

MY RATING ☆ ☆ ☆ ☆ ☆ NUMBER OF NIGHTS HERE ......

WEATHER .... TEMPERATURE ....

WILDCAMPING LOCATION NOTES

....

....

....

....

.... GPS ....

DAILY COSTS		TODAY'S HIGHLIGHTS
SITE FEES	£	....
FUEL	£	....
PROPANE	£	....
TOLLS	£	....
GROCERIES	£	....
DINING OUT	£	....
ENTERTAINMENT	£	....
OTHER COSTS	£	....

TO DO TOMORROW

....

....

....

....

NOTES

....

....

....

....

....

....

....

....

SKETCH / KEEPSAKE / PHOTOGRAPH

MOTORHOME
ROAD TRIP TRAVEL JOURNAL

DATE .... MILEAGE START ....

START TIME .... MILEAGE END ....

ARRIVAL TIME .... MILEAGE TOTAL ....

CAMPSITE NAME ....

ADDRESS 1 ....

ADDRESS 2 ....

POST CODE .... GPS ....

E MAIL .... PHONE ....

WEBSITE WWW..

MY RATING ☆ ☆ ☆ ☆ ☆ NUMBER OF NIGHTS HERE ......

WEATHER .... TEMPERATURE ....

WILDCAMPING LOCATION NOTES

....
....
....
.... GPS ....

DAILY COSTS		TODAY'S HIGHLIGHTS
SITE FEES	£	....
FUEL	£	....
PROPANE	£	....
TOLLS	£	....
GROCERIES	£	....
DINING OUT	£	....
ENTERTAINMENT	£	....
OTHER COSTS	£	....

TO DO TOMORROW

....

....

....

....

NOTES

....

....

....

....

....

....

....

SKETCH / KEEPSAKE / PHOTOGRAPH

MOTORHOME
ROAD TRIP TRAVEL JOURNAL

DATE .... MILEAGE START ....

START TIME .... MILEAGE END ....

ARRIVAL TIME .... MILEAGE TOTAL ....

CAMPSITE NAME ....

ADDRESS 1 ....

ADDRESS 2 ....

POST CODE .... GPS ....

E MAIL .... PHONE ....

WEBSITE WWW...

MY RATING ☆ ☆ ☆ ☆ ☆ NUMBER OF NIGHTS HERE ......

WEATHER .... TEMPERATURE ....

WILDCAMPING LOCATION NOTES

....

....

....

....

.... GPS ....

DAILY COSTS		TODAY'S HIGHLIGHTS
SITE FEES	£	....
FUEL	£	....
PROPANE	£	....
TOLLS	£	....
GROCERIES	£	....
DINING OUT	£	....
ENTERTAINMENT	£	....
OTHER COSTS	£	....

TO DO TOMORROW

....

....

....

....

NOTES

....

....

....

....

....

....

....

....

SKETCH / KEEPSAKE / PHOTOGRAPH

MOTORHOME
ROAD TRIP TRAVEL JOURNAL

DATE .... MILEAGE START ....

START TIME .... MILEAGE END ....

ARRIVAL TIME .... MILEAGE TOTAL ....

CAMPSITE NAME ....

ADDRESS 1 ....

ADDRESS 2 ....

POST CODE .... GPS ....

E MAIL .... PHONE ....

WEBSITE WWW..

MY RATING ☆ ☆ ☆ ☆ ☆ NUMBER OF NIGHTS HERE ......

WEATHER .... TEMPERATURE ....

WILDCAMPING LOCATION NOTES

....
....
....
....
.... GPS ....

DAILY COSTS		TODAY'S HIGHLIGHTS
SITE FEES	£	....
FUEL	£	....
PROPANE	£	....
TOLLS	£	....
GROCERIES	£	....
DINING OUT	£	....
ENTERTAINMENT	£	....
OTHER COSTS	£	....

TO DO TOMORROW

....

....

....

....

NOTES

....

....

....

....

....

....

....

....

SKETCH / KEEPSAKE / PHOTOGRAPH

MOTORHOME
ROAD TRIP TRAVEL JOURNAL

DATE .... MILEAGE START ....

START TIME .... MILEAGE END ....

ARRIVAL TIME .... MILEAGE TOTAL ....

CAMPSITE NAME ....

ADDRESS 1 ....

ADDRESS 2 ....

POST CODE .... GPS ....

E MAIL .... PHONE ....

WEBSITE WWW...

MY RATING ☆ ☆ ☆ ☆ ☆ NUMBER OF NIGHTS HERE ......

WEATHER .... TEMPERATURE ....

WILDCAMPING LOCATION NOTES

....
....
....
.... GPS ....

DAILY COSTS		TODAY'S HIGHLIGHTS
SITE FEES	£	....
FUEL	£	....
PROPANE	£	....
TOLLS	£	....
GROCERIES	£	....
DINING OUT	£	....
ENTERTAINMENT	£	....
OTHER COSTS	£	....

TO DO TOMORROW

....
....
....
....

NOTES

....

....

....

....

....

....

....

....

SKETCH / KEEPSAKE / PHOTOGRAPH

MOTORHOME
ROAD TRIP TRAVEL JOURNAL

DATE .... MILEAGE START ....

START TIME .... MILEAGE END ....

ARRIVAL TIME .... MILEAGE TOTAL ....

CAMPSITE NAME ....

ADDRESS I ....

ADDRESS 2 ....

POST CODE .... GPS ....

E MAIL .... PHONE ....

WEBSITE WWW...

MY RATING ☆ ☆ ☆ ☆ ☆ NUMBER OF NIGHTS HERE ......

WEATHER .... TEMPERATURE ....

WILDCAMPING LOCATION NOTES

....

....

....

.... GPS ....

DAILY COSTS		TODAY'S HIGHLIGHTS
SITE FEES	£	....
FUEL	£	....
PROPANE	£	....
TOLLS	£	....
GROCERIES	£	....
DINING OUT	£	....
ENTERTAINMENT	£	....
OTHER COSTS	£	....

TO DO TOMORROW

....

....

....

....

NOTES

....

....

....

....

....

....

....

....

SKETCH / KEEPSAKE / PHOTOGRAPH

MOTORHOME
ROAD TRIP TRAVEL JOURNAL

DATE .... MILEAGE START ....

START TIME .... MILEAGE END ....

ARRIVAL TIME .... MILEAGE TOTAL ....

CAMPSITE NAME ....

ADDRESS 1 ....

ADDRESS 2 ....

POST CODE .... GPS ....

E MAIL .... PHONE ....

WEBSITE WWW...

MY RATING ☆ ☆ ☆ ☆ ☆ NUMBER OF NIGHTS HERE ......

WEATHER .... TEMPERATURE ....

WILDCAMPING LOCATION NOTES

....
....
....
....
.... GPS ....

DAILY COSTS

SITE FEES £ ....

FUEL £ ....

PROPANE £ ....

TOLLS £ ....

GROCERIES £ ....

DINING OUT £ ....

ENTERTAINMENT £ ....

OTHER COSTS £ ....

TODAY'S HIGHLIGHTS

....
....
....
....
....
....
....
....

TO DO TOMORROW

....
....
....
....

NOTES

....

....

....

....

....

....

....

....

SKETCH / KEEPSAKE / PHOTOGRAPH

MOTORHOME
ROAD TRIP TRAVEL JOURNAL

DATE .... MILEAGE START ....

START TIME .... MILEAGE END ....

ARRIVAL TIME .... MILEAGE TOTAL ....

CAMPSITE NAME ....

ADDRESS 1 ....

ADDRESS 2 ....

POST CODE .... GPS ....

E MAIL .... PHONE ....

WEBSITE WWW...

MY RATING ☆ ☆ ☆ ☆ ☆ NUMBER OF NIGHTS HERE ......

WEATHER .... TEMPERATURE ....

WILDCAMPING LOCATION NOTES

....
....
....
.... GPS ....

DAILY COSTS		TODAY'S HIGHLIGHTS
SITE FEES	£	....
FUEL	£	....
PROPANE	£	....
TOLLS	£	....
GROCERIES	£	....
DINING OUT	£	....
ENTERTAINMENT	£	....
OTHER COSTS	£	....

TO DO TOMORROW

....

....

....

....

NOTES

....

....

....

....

....

....

....

....

SKETCH / KEEPSAKE / PHOTOGRAPH

MOTORHOME
ROAD TRIP TRAVEL JOURNAL

DATE .... MILEAGE START ....

START TIME .... MILEAGE END ....

ARRIVAL TIME .... MILEAGE TOTAL ....

CAMPSITE NAME ....

ADDRESS 1 ....

ADDRESS 2 ....

POST CODE .... GPS ....

E MAIL .... PHONE ....

WEBSITE WWW..

MY RATING ☆ ☆ ☆ ☆ ☆ NUMBER OF NIGHTS HERE ......

WEATHER .... TEMPERATURE ....

WILDCAMPING LOCATION NOTES

....
....
....
.... GPS ....

DAILY COSTS		TODAY'S HIGHLIGHTS
SITE FEES	£	....
FUEL	£	....
PROPANE	£	....
TOLLS	£	....
GROCERIES	£	....
DINING OUT	£	....
ENTERTAINMENT	£	....
OTHER COSTS	£	....

TO DO TOMORROW

....

....

....

....

NOTES

....

....

....

....

....

....

....

....

SKETCH / KEEPSAKE / PHOTOGRAPH

MOTORHOME
ROAD TRIP TRAVEL JOURNAL

DATE .... MILEAGE START ....

START TIME .... MILEAGE END ....

ARRIVAL TIME .... MILEAGE TOTAL ....

CAMPSITE NAME ....

ADDRESS 1 ....

ADDRESS 2 ....

POST CODE .... GPS ....

E MAIL .... PHONE ....

WEBSITE WWW...

MY RATING ☆ ☆ ☆ ☆ ☆ NUMBER OF NIGHTS HERE ......

WEATHER .... TEMPERATURE ....

WILDCAMPING LOCATION NOTES

....
....
....
.... GPS ....

DAILY COSTS		TODAY'S HIGHLIGHTS
SITE FEES	£	....
FUEL	£	....
PROPANE	£	....
TOLLS	£	....
GROCERIES	£	....
DINING OUT	£	....
ENTERTAINMENT	£	....
OTHER COSTS	£	....

TO DO TOMORROW

....

....

....

....

NOTES

....

....

....

....

....

....

....

SKETCH / KEEPSAKE / PHOTOGRAPH

MOTORHOME
ROAD TRIP TRAVEL JOURNAL

DATE .... MILEAGE START ....

START TIME .... MILEAGE END ....

ARRIVAL TIME .... MILEAGE TOTAL ....

CAMPSITE NAME ....

ADDRESS 1 ....

ADDRESS 2 ....

POST CODE .... GPS ....

E MAIL .... PHONE ....

WEBSITE WWW...

MY RATING ☆ ☆ ☆ ☆ ☆ NUMBER OF NIGHTS HERE ......

WEATHER .... TEMPERATURE ....

WILDCAMPING LOCATION NOTES

....

....

....

.... GPS ....

DAILY COSTS		TODAY'S HIGHLIGHTS
SITE FEES	£	....
FUEL	£	....
PROPANE	£	....
TOLLS	£	....
GROCERIES	£	....
DINING OUT	£	....
ENTERTAINMENT	£	....
OTHER COSTS	£	....

TO DO TOMORROW

....

....

....

....

NOTES

....

....

....

....

....

....

....

SKETCH / KEEPSAKE / PHOTOGRAPH

MOTORHOME
ROAD TRIP TRAVEL JOURNAL

DATE .... MILEAGE START ....

START TIME .... MILEAGE END ....

ARRIVAL TIME .... MILEAGE TOTAL ....

CAMPSITE NAME ....

ADDRESS 1 ....

ADDRESS 2 ....

POST CODE .... GPS ....

E MAIL .... PHONE ....

WEBSITE WWW...

MY RATING ☆ ☆ ☆ ☆ ☆ NUMBER OF NIGHTS HERE ......

WEATHER .... TEMPERATURE ....

WILDCAMPING LOCATION NOTES

....
....
....
.... GPS ....

DAILY COSTS	TODAY'S HIGHLIGHTS
SITE FEES £	....
FUEL £	....
PROPANE £	....
TOLLS £	....
GROCERIES £	....
DINING OUT £	....
ENTERTAINMENT £	....
OTHER COSTS £	....

TO DO TOMORROW

....

....

....

....

NOTES

....

....

....

....

....

....

....

....

SKETCH / KEEPSAKE / PHOTOGRAPH

MOTORHOME
ROAD TRIP TRAVEL JOURNAL

DATE .... MILEAGE START ....

START TIME .... MILEAGE END ....

ARRIVAL TIME .... MILEAGE TOTAL ....

CAMPSITE NAME ....

ADDRESS 1 ....

ADDRESS 2 ....

POST CODE .... GPS ....

E MAIL .... PHONE ....

WEBSITE WWW...

MY RATING ☆ ☆ ☆ ☆ NUMBER OF NIGHTS HERE ......

WEATHER .... TEMPERATURE ....

WILDCAMPING LOCATION NOTES

....
....
....
....
.... GPS ....

DAILY COSTS   TODAY'S HIGHLIGHTS

SITE FEES   £ ....

FUEL   £ ....

PROPANE   £ ....

TOLLS   £ ....

GROCERIES   £ ....

DINING OUT   £ ....

ENTERTAINMENT £ ....

OTHER COSTS   £ ....

TO DO TOMORROW

....

....

....

....

NOTES

....

....

....

....

....

....

....

SKETCH / KEEPSAKE / PHOTOGRAPH

MOTORHOME
ROAD TRIP TRAVEL JOURNAL

DATE .... MILEAGE START ....

START TIME .... MILEAGE END ....

ARRIVAL TIME .... MILEAGE TOTAL ....

CAMPSITE NAME ....

ADDRESS 1 ....

ADDRESS 2 ....

POST CODE .... GPS ....

E MAIL .... PHONE ....

WEBSITE WWW..

MY RATING ☆ ☆ ☆ ☆ ☆ NUMBER OF NIGHTS HERE ......

WEATHER .... TEMPERATURE ....

WILDCAMPING LOCATION NOTES

....
....
....
.... GPS ....

DAILY COSTS		TODAY'S HIGHLIGHTS
SITE FEES	£	....
FUEL	£	....
PROPANE	£	....
TOLLS	£	....
GROCERIES	£	....
DINING OUT	£	....
ENTERTAINMENT	£	....
OTHER COSTS	£	....

TO DO TOMORROW

....

....

....

....

NOTES

....

....

....

....

....

....

....

SKETCH / KEEPSAKE / PHOTOGRAPH

MOTORHOME
ROAD TRIP TRAVEL JOURNAL

DATE .... MILEAGE START ....

START TIME .... MILEAGE END ....

ARRIVAL TIME .... MILEAGE TOTAL ....

CAMPSITE NAME ....

ADDRESS 1 ....

ADDRESS 2 ....

POST CODE .... GPS ....

E MAIL .... PHONE ....

WEBSITE WWW...

MY RATING ☆ ☆ ☆ ☆ ☆ NUMBER OF NIGHTS HERE ......

WEATHER .... TEMPERATURE ....

WILDCAMPING LOCATION NOTES

....
....
....
....
.... GPS ....

DAILY COSTS	TODAY'S HIGHLIGHTS
SITE FEES £	....
FUEL £	....
PROPANE £	....
TOLLS £	....
GROCERIES £	....
DINING OUT £	....
ENTERTAINMENT £	....
OTHER COSTS £	....

TO DO TOMORROW

....

....

....

....

NOTES

....

....

....

....

....

....

....

....

SKETCH / KEEPSAKE / PHOTOGRAPH

MOTORHOME
ROAD TRIP TRAVEL JOURNAL

DATE .... MILEAGE START ....

START TIME .... MILEAGE END ....

ARRIVAL TIME .... MILEAGE TOTAL ....

CAMPSITE NAME ....

ADDRESS 1 ....

ADDRESS 2 ....

POST CODE .... GPS ....

E MAIL .... PHONE ....

WEBSITE WWW..

MY RATING ☆ ☆ ☆ ☆ ☆ NUMBER OF NIGHTS HERE ......

WEATHER .... TEMPERATURE ....

WILDCAMPING LOCATION NOTES

....
....
....
....
.... GPS ....

DAILY COSTS	TODAY'S HIGHLIGHTS
SITE FEES £	....
FUEL £	....
PROPANE £	....
TOLLS £	....
GROCERIES £	....
DINING OUT £	....
ENTERTAINMENT £	....
OTHER COSTS £	....

TO DO TOMORROW

....

....

....

....

NOTES

....

....

....

....

....

....

....

....

SKETCH / KEEPSAKE / PHOTOGRAPH

MOTORHOME
ROAD TRIP TRAVEL JOURNAL

DATE .... MILEAGE START ....

START TIME .... MILEAGE END ....

ARRIVAL TIME .... MILEAGE TOTAL ....

CAMPSITE NAME ....

ADDRESS 1 ....

ADDRESS 2 ....

POST CODE .... GPS ....

E MAIL .... PHONE ....

WEBSITE WWW...

MY RATING ☆ ☆ ☆ ☆ ☆ NUMBER OF NIGHTS HERE ......

WEATHER .... TEMPERATURE ....

WILDCAMPING LOCATION NOTES

....
....
....
.... GPS ....

DAILY COSTS		TODAY'S HIGHLIGHTS
SITE FEES	£	....
FUEL	£	....
PROPANE	£	....
TOLLS	£	....
GROCERIES	£	....
DINING OUT	£	....
ENTERTAINMENT	£	....
OTHER COSTS	£	....

TO DO TOMORROW

....

....

....

....

NOTES

....

....

....

....

....

....

....

....

SKETCH / KEEPSAKE / PHOTOGRAPH

MOTORHOME
ROAD TRIP TRAVEL JOURNAL

DATE .... MILEAGE START ....

START TIME .... MILEAGE END ....

ARRIVAL TIME .... MILEAGE TOTAL ....

CAMPSITE NAME ....

ADDRESS I ....

ADDRESS 2 ....

POST CODE .... GPS ....

E MAIL .... PHONE ....

WEBSITE WWW...

MY RATING ☆ ☆ ☆ ☆ ☆ NUMBER OF NIGHTS HERE ......

WEATHER .... TEMPERATURE ....

WILDCAMPING LOCATION NOTES

....
....
....
....
.... GPS ....

DAILY COSTS	TODAY'S HIGHLIGHTS
SITE FEES £	....
FUEL £	....
PROPANE £	....
TOLLS £	....
GROCERIES £	....
DINING OUT £	....
ENTERTAINMENT £	....
OTHER COSTS £	....

TO DO TOMORROW

....

....

....

....

NOTES

....

....

....

....

....

....

....

....

SKETCH / KEEPSAKE / PHOTOGRAPH

MOTORHOME
ROAD TRIP TRAVEL JOURNAL

DATE .... MILEAGE START ....

START TIME .... MILEAGE END ....

ARRIVAL TIME .... MILEAGE TOTAL ....

CAMPSITE NAME ....

ADDRESS 1 ....

ADDRESS 2 ....

POST CODE .... GPS ....

E MAIL .... PHONE ....

WEBSITE WWW...

MY RATING ☆ ☆ ☆ ☆ ☆ NUMBER OF NIGHTS HERE ......

WEATHER .... TEMPERATURE ....

WILDCAMPING LOCATION NOTES

....
....
....
....
.... GPS ....

DAILY COSTS   TODAY'S HIGHLIGHTS

SITE FEES   £ ....

FUEL   £ ....

PROPANE   £ ....

TOLLS   £ ....

GROCERIES   £ ....

DINING OUT   £ ....

ENTERTAINMENT £ ....

OTHER COSTS   £ ....

TO DO TOMORROW

....

....

....

....

NOTES

....

....

....

....

....

....

....

SKETCH / KEEPSAKE / PHOTOGRAPH

MOTORHOME
ROAD TRIP TRAVEL JOURNAL

DATE .... MILEAGE START ....

START TIME .... MILEAGE END ....

ARRIVAL TIME .... MILEAGE TOTAL ....

CAMPSITE NAME ....

ADDRESS 1 ....

ADDRESS 2 ....

POST CODE .... GPS ....

E MAIL .... PHONE ....

WEBSITE WWW..

MY RATING ☆ ☆ ☆ ☆ ☆ NUMBER OF NIGHTS HERE ......

WEATHER .... TEMPERATURE ....

WILDCAMPING LOCATION NOTES

....
....
....
.... GPS ....

DAILY COSTS	TODAY'S HIGHLIGHTS
SITE FEES £	....
FUEL £	....
PROPANE £	....
TOLLS £	....
GROCERIES £	....
DINING OUT £	....
ENTERTAINMENT £	....
OTHER COSTS £	....

TO DO TOMORROW

....
....
....
....

NOTES

....

....

....

....

....

....

....

SKETCH / KEEPSAKE / PHOTOGRAPH

MOTORHOME
ROAD TRIP TRAVEL JOURNAL

DATE .... MILEAGE START ....

START TIME .... MILEAGE END ....

ARRIVAL TIME .... MILEAGE TOTAL ....

CAMPSITE NAME ....

ADDRESS 1 ....

ADDRESS 2 ....

POST CODE .... GPS ....

E MAIL .... PHONE ....

WEBSITE WWW..

MY RATING ☆ ☆ ☆ ☆ ☆ NUMBER OF NIGHTS HERE ......

WEATHER .... TEMPERATURE ....

WILDCAMPING LOCATION NOTES

....
....
....
.... GPS ....

DAILY COSTS	TODAY'S HIGHLIGHTS
SITE FEES £	....
FUEL £	....
PROPANE £	....
TOLLS £	....
GROCERIES £	....
DINING OUT £	....
ENTERTAINMENT £	....
OTHER COSTS £	....

TO DO TOMORROW

....

....

....

....

NOTES

....

....

....

....

....

....

....

....

SKETCH / KEEPSAKE / PHOTOGRAPH

MOTORHOME
ROAD TRIP TRAVEL JOURNAL

DATE .... MILEAGE START ....

START TIME .... MILEAGE END ....

ARRIVAL TIME .... MILEAGE TOTAL ....

CAMPSITE NAME ....

ADDRESS 1 ....

ADDRESS 2 ....

POST CODE .... GPS ....

E MAIL .... PHONE ....

WEBSITE WWW...

MY RATING ☆ ☆ ☆ ☆ ☆ NUMBER OF NIGHTS HERE ......

WEATHER .... TEMPERATURE ....

WILDCAMPING LOCATION NOTES

....
....
....
....
.... GPS ....

DAILY COSTS

TODAY'S HIGHLIGHTS

SITE FEES £ ....

FUEL £ ....

PROPANE £ ....

TOLLS £ ....

GROCERIES £ ....

DINING OUT £ ....

ENTERTAINMENT £ ....

OTHER COSTS £ ....

TO DO TOMORROW

....
....
....
....

NOTES

....

....

....

....

....

....

....

SKETCH / KEEPSAKE / PHOTOGRAPH

MOTORHOME
ROAD TRIP TRAVEL JOURNAL

DATE .... MILEAGE START ....

START TIME .... MILEAGE END ....

ARRIVAL TIME .... MILEAGE TOTAL ....

CAMPSITE NAME ....

ADDRESS 1 ....

ADDRESS 2 ....

POST CODE .... GPS ....

E MAIL .... PHONE ....

WEBSITE WWW...

MY RATING ☆ ☆ ☆ ☆ ☆ NUMBER OF NIGHTS HERE ......

WEATHER .... TEMPERATURE ....

WILDCAMPING LOCATION NOTES

....

....

....

.... GPS ....

DAILY COSTS		TODAY'S HIGHLIGHTS
SITE FEES	£	....
FUEL	£	....
PROPANE	£	....
TOLLS	£	....
GROCERIES	£	....
DINING OUT	£	....
ENTERTAINMENT	£	....
OTHER COSTS	£	....

TO DO TOMORROW

....

....

....

....

NOTES

....

....

....

....

....

....

....

....

SKETCH / KEEPSAKE / PHOTOGRAPH

MOTORHOME
ROAD TRIP TRAVEL JOURNAL

DATE .... MILEAGE START ....

START TIME .... MILEAGE END ....

ARRIVAL TIME .... MILEAGE TOTAL ....

CAMPSITE NAME ....

ADDRESS 1 ....

ADDRESS 2 ....

POST CODE .... GPS ....

E MAIL .... PHONE ....

WEBSITE WWW...

MY RATING ☆ ☆ ☆ ☆ ☆ NUMBER OF NIGHTS HERE ......

WEATHER .... TEMPERATURE ....

WILDCAMPING LOCATION NOTES

....
....
....
....
.... GPS ....

DAILY COSTS	TODAY'S HIGHLIGHTS
SITE FEES £	....
FUEL £	....
PROPANE £	....
TOLLS £	....
GROCERIES £	....
DINING OUT £	....
ENTERTAINMENT £	....
OTHER COSTS £	....

TO DO TOMORROW

....

....

....

....

NOTES

....

....

....

....

....

....

....

....

SKETCH / KEEPSAKE / PHOTOGRAPH

MOTORHOME
ROAD TRIP TRAVEL JOURNAL

DATE .... MILEAGE START ....

START TIME .... MILEAGE END ....

ARRIVAL TIME .... MILEAGE TOTAL ....

CAMPSITE NAME ....

ADDRESS 1 ....

ADDRESS 2 ....

POST CODE .... GPS ....

E MAIL .... PHONE ....

WEBSITE WWW..

MY RATING ☆ ☆ ☆ ☆ ☆ NUMBER OF NIGHTS HERE ......

WEATHER .... TEMPERATURE ....

WILDCAMPING LOCATION NOTES

....
....
....
....
.... GPS ....

DAILY COSTS		TODAY'S HIGHLIGHTS
SITE FEES	£	....
FUEL	£	....
PROPANE	£	....
TOLLS	£	....
GROCERIES	£	....
DINING OUT	£	....
ENTERTAINMENT	£	....
OTHER COSTS	£	....

TO DO TOMORROW

....

....

....

....

NOTES

....

....

....

....

....

....

....

SKETCH / KEEPSAKE / PHOTOGRAPH

MOTORHOME
ROAD TRIP TRAVEL JOURNAL

DATE .... MILEAGE START ....

START TIME .... MILEAGE END ....

ARRIVAL TIME .... MILEAGE TOTAL ....

CAMPSITE NAME ....

ADDRESS 1 ....

ADDRESS 2 ....

POST CODE .... GPS ....

E MAIL .... PHONE ....

WEBSITE WWW..

MY RATING ☆ ☆ ☆ ☆ ☆ NUMBER OF NIGHTS HERE ......

WEATHER .... TEMPERATURE ....

WILDCAMPING LOCATION NOTES

....
....
....
.... GPS ....

DAILY COSTS	TODAY'S HIGHLIGHTS
SITE FEES £	....
FUEL £	....
PROPANE £	....
TOLLS £	....
GROCERIES £	....
DINING OUT £	....
ENTERTAINMENT £	....
OTHER COSTS £	....

TO DO TOMORROW

....

....

....

....

NOTES

....

....

....

....

....

....

....

SKETCH / KEEPSAKE / PHOTOGRAPH

MOTORHOME
ROAD TRIP TRAVEL JOURNAL

DATE .... MILEAGE START ....

START TIME .... MILEAGE END ....

ARRIVAL TIME .... MILEAGE TOTAL ....

CAMPSITE NAME ....

ADDRESS 1 ....

ADDRESS 2 ....

POST CODE .... GPS ....

E MAIL .... PHONE ....

WEBSITE WWW...

MY RATING ☆ ☆ ☆ ☆ ☆ NUMBER OF NIGHTS HERE ......

WEATHER .... TEMPERATURE ....

WILDCAMPING LOCATION NOTES

....
....
....
.... GPS ....

DAILY COSTS	TODAY'S HIGHLIGHTS
SITE FEES £	....
FUEL £	....
PROPANE £	....
TOLLS £	....
GROCERIES £	....
DINING OUT £	....
ENTERTAINMENT £	....
OTHER COSTS £	....

TO DO TOMORROW

....

....

....

....

NOTES

....

....

....

....

....

....

....

SKETCH / KEEPSAKE / PHOTOGRAPH

MOTORHOME
ROAD TRIP TRAVEL JOURNAL

DATE .... MILEAGE START ....

START TIME .... MILEAGE END ....

ARRIVAL TIME .... MILEAGE TOTAL ....

CAMPSITE NAME ....

ADDRESS 1 ....

ADDRESS 2 ....

POST CODE .... GPS ....

E MAIL .... PHONE ....

WEBSITE WWW..

MY RATING ☆ ☆ ☆ ☆ ☆ NUMBER OF NIGHTS HERE ......

WEATHER .... TEMPERATURE ....

WILDCAMPING LOCATION NOTES

....
....
....
....
.... GPS ....

DAILY COSTS		TODAY'S HIGHLIGHTS
SITE FEES	£	....
FUEL	£	....
PROPANE	£	....
TOLLS	£	....
GROCERIES	£	....
DINING OUT	£	....
ENTERTAINMENT	£	....
OTHER COSTS	£	....

TO DO TOMORROW

....

....

....

....

NOTES

....

....

....

....

....

....

....

....

SKETCH / KEEPSAKE / PHOTOGRAPH

MOTORHOME
ROAD TRIP TRAVEL JOURNAL

DATE .... MILEAGE START ....

START TIME .... MILEAGE END ....

ARRIVAL TIME .... MILEAGE TOTAL ....

CAMPSITE NAME ....

ADDRESS 1 ....

ADDRESS 2 ....

POST CODE .... GPS ....

E MAIL .... PHONE ....

WEBSITE WWW...

MY RATING ☆ ☆ ☆ ☆ ☆ NUMBER OF NIGHTS HERE ......

WEATHER .... TEMPERATURE ....

WILDCAMPING LOCATION NOTES

....
....
....
.... GPS ....

DAILY COSTS		TODAY'S HIGHLIGHTS
SITE FEES	£	....
FUEL	£	....
PROPANE	£	....
TOLLS	£	....
GROCERIES	£	....
DINING OUT	£	....
ENTERTAINMENT	£	....
OTHER COSTS	£	....

TO DO TOMORROW

....

....

....

....

NOTES

....

....

....

....

....

....

....

....

SKETCH / KEEPSAKE / PHOTOGRAPH

MOTORHOME
ROAD TRIP TRAVEL JOURNAL

DATE .... MILEAGE START ....

START TIME .... MILEAGE END ....

ARRIVAL TIME .... MILEAGE TOTAL ....

CAMPSITE NAME ....

ADDRESS 1 ....

ADDRESS 2 ....

POST CODE .... GPS ....

E MAIL .... PHONE ....

WEBSITE WWW..

MY RATING ☆ ☆ ☆ ☆ ☆ NUMBER OF NIGHTS HERE ......

WEATHER .... TEMPERATURE ....

WILDCAMPING LOCATION NOTES

....

....

....

....

.... GPS ....

DAILY COSTS	TODAY'S HIGHLIGHTS
SITE FEES £	....
FUEL £	....
PROPANE £	....
TOLLS £	....
GROCERIES £	....
DINING OUT £	....
ENTERTAINMENT £	....
OTHER COSTS £	....

TO DO TOMORROW

....

....

....

....

NOTES

....

....

....

....

....

....

....

SKETCH / KEEPSAKE / PHOTOGRAPH

MOTORHOME
ROAD TRIP TRAVEL JOURNAL

DATE .... MILEAGE START ....

START TIME .... MILEAGE END ....

ARRIVAL TIME .... MILEAGE TOTAL ....

CAMPSITE NAME ....

ADDRESS 1 ....

ADDRESS 2 ....

POST CODE .... GPS ....

E MAIL .... PHONE ....

WEBSITE WWW...

MY RATING ☆ ☆ ☆ ☆ ☆ NUMBER OF NIGHTS HERE ......

WEATHER .... TEMPERATURE ....

WILDCAMPING LOCATION NOTES

....

....

....

....

.... GPS ....

DAILY COSTS		TODAY'S HIGHLIGHTS
SITE FEES	£	....
FUEL	£	....
PROPANE	£	....
TOLLS	£	....
GROCERIES	£	....
DINING OUT	£	....
ENTERTAINMENT	£	....
OTHER COSTS	£	....

TO DO TOMORROW

....

....

....

....

NOTES

....

....

....

....

....

....

....

....

SKETCH / KEEPSAKE / PHOTOGRAPH

MOTORHOME
ROAD TRIP TRAVEL JOURNAL

DATE .... MILEAGE START ....

START TIME .... MILEAGE END ....

ARRIVAL TIME .... MILEAGE TOTAL ....

CAMPSITE NAME ....

ADDRESS 1 ....

ADDRESS 2 ....

POST CODE .... GPS ....

E MAIL .... PHONE ....

WEBSITE WWW...

MY RATING ☆ ☆ ☆ ☆ ☆ NUMBER OF NIGHTS HERE ......

WEATHER .... TEMPERATURE ....

WILDCAMPING LOCATION NOTES

....
....
....
....
.... GPS ....

DAILY COSTS		TODAY'S HIGHLIGHTS
SITE FEES	£	....
FUEL	£	....
PROPANE	£	....
TOLLS	£	....
GROCERIES	£	....
DINING OUT	£	....
ENTERTAINMENT	£	....
OTHER COSTS	£	....

TO DO TOMORROW

....

....

....

....

NOTES

....

....

....

....

....

....

....

....

SKETCH / KEEPSAKE / PHOTOGRAPH

MOTORHOME
ROAD TRIP TRAVEL JOURNAL

DATE .... MILEAGE START ....

START TIME .... MILEAGE END ....

ARRIVAL TIME .... MILEAGE TOTAL ....

CAMPSITE NAME ....

ADDRESS 1 ....

ADDRESS 2 ....

POST CODE .... GPS ....

E MAIL .... PHONE ....

WEBSITE WWW..

MY RATING ☆ ☆ ☆ ☆ ☆ NUMBER OF NIGHTS HERE ......

WEATHER .... TEMPERATURE ....

WILDCAMPING LOCATION NOTES

....
....
....
....
.... GPS ....

DAILY COSTS	TODAY'S HIGHLIGHTS
SITE FEES £	....
FUEL £	....
PROPANE £	....
TOLLS £	....
GROCERIES £	....
DINING OUT £	....
ENTERTAINMENT £	....
OTHER COSTS £	....

TO DO TOMORROW

....

....

....

....

NOTES

....

....

....

....

....

....

....

SKETCH / KEEPSAKE / PHOTOGRAPH

MOTORHOME
ROAD TRIP TRAVEL JOURNAL

DATE .... MILEAGE START ....

START TIME .... MILEAGE END ....

ARRIVAL TIME .... MILEAGE TOTAL ....

CAMPSITE NAME ....

ADDRESS 1 ....

ADDRESS 2 ....

POST CODE .... GPS ....

E MAIL .... PHONE ....

WEBSITE WWW...

MY RATING ☆ ☆ ☆ ☆ ☆ NUMBER OF NIGHTS HERE ......

WEATHER .... TEMPERATURE ....

WILDCAMPING LOCATION NOTES

....
....
....
....
.... GPS ....

DAILY COSTS		TODAY'S HIGHLIGHTS
SITE FEES	£	....
FUEL	£	....
PROPANE	£	....
TOLLS	£	....
GROCERIES	£	....
DINING OUT	£	....
ENTERTAINMENT	£	....
OTHER COSTS	£	....

TO DO TOMORROW

....
....
....
....

NOTES

....

....

....

....

....

....

....

....

SKETCH / KEEPSAKE / PHOTOGRAPH

MOTORHOME
ROAD TRIP TRAVEL JOURNAL

DATE .... MILEAGE START ....

START TIME .... MILEAGE END ....

ARRIVAL TIME .... MILEAGE TOTAL ....

CAMPSITE NAME ....

ADDRESS 1 ....

ADDRESS 2 ....

POST CODE .... GPS ....

E MAIL .... PHONE ....

WEBSITE WWW...

MY RATING ☆ ☆ ☆ ☆ ☆ NUMBER OF NIGHTS HERE ......

WEATHER .... TEMPERATURE ....

WILDCAMPING LOCATION NOTES

....

....

....

....

.... GPS ....

DAILY COSTS	TODAY'S HIGHLIGHTS
SITE FEES £	....
FUEL £	....
PROPANE £	....
TOLLS £	....
GROCERIES £	....
DINING OUT £	....
ENTERTAINMENT £	....
OTHER COSTS £	....

TO DO TOMORROW

....

....

....

....

NOTES

....

....

....

....

....

....

....

....

SKETCH / KEEPSAKE / PHOTOGRAPH

MOTORHOME
ROAD TRIP TRAVEL JOURNAL

DATE .... MILEAGE START ....

START TIME .... MILEAGE END ....

ARRIVAL TIME .... MILEAGE TOTAL ....

CAMPSITE NAME ....

ADDRESS 1 ....

ADDRESS 2 ....

POST CODE .... GPS ....

E MAIL .... PHONE ....

WEBSITE WWW...

MY RATING ☆ ☆ ☆ ☆ ☆ NUMBER OF NIGHTS HERE ......

WEATHER .... TEMPERATURE ....

WILDCAMPING LOCATION NOTES

....
....
....
....
.... GPS ....

DAILY COSTS		TODAY'S HIGHLIGHTS
SITE FEES	£	....
FUEL	£	....
PROPANE	£	....
TOLLS	£	....
GROCERIES	£	....
DINING OUT	£	....
ENTERTAINMENT	£	....
OTHER COSTS	£	....

TO DO TOMORROW

....

....

....

....

NOTES

....

....

....

....

....

....

....

SKETCH / KEEPSAKE / PHOTOGRAPH

MOTORHOME
ROAD TRIP TRAVEL JOURNAL

DATE .... MILEAGE START ....

START TIME .... MILEAGE END ....

ARRIVAL TIME .... MILEAGE TOTAL ....

CAMPSITE NAME ....

ADDRESS 1 ....

ADDRESS 2 ....

POST CODE .... GPS ....

E MAIL .... PHONE ....

WEBSITE WWW...

MY RATING ☆ ☆ ☆ ☆ ☆ NUMBER OF NIGHTS HERE ......

WEATHER .... TEMPERATURE ....

WILDCAMPING LOCATION NOTES

....

....

....

....

.... GPS ....

DAILY COSTS		TODAY'S HIGHLIGHTS
SITE FEES	£	....
FUEL	£	....
PROPANE	£	....
TOLLS	£	....
GROCERIES	£	....
DINING OUT	£	....
ENTERTAINMENT	£	....
OTHER COSTS	£	....

TO DO TOMORROW

....

....

....

....

NOTES

....

....

....

....

....

....

....

....

SKETCH / KEEPSAKE / PHOTOGRAPH

MOTORHOME
ROAD TRIP TRAVEL JOURNAL

DATE .... MILEAGE START ....

START TIME .... MILEAGE END ....

ARRIVAL TIME .... MILEAGE TOTAL ....

CAMPSITE NAME ....

ADDRESS 1 ....

ADDRESS 2 ....

POST CODE .... GPS ....

E MAIL .... PHONE ....

WEBSITE WWW..

MY RATING ☆ ☆ ☆ ☆ ☆ NUMBER OF NIGHTS HERE ......

WEATHER .... TEMPERATURE ....

WILDCAMPING LOCATION NOTES

....
....
....
.... GPS ....

DAILY COSTS		TODAY'S HIGHLIGHTS
SITE FEES	£	....
FUEL	£	....
PROPANE	£	....
TOLLS	£	....
GROCERIES	£	....
DINING OUT	£	....
ENTERTAINMENT	£	....
OTHER COSTS	£	....

TO DO TOMORROW

....
....
....
....

NOTES

....

....

....

....

....

....

....

SKETCH / KEEPSAKE / PHOTOGRAPH

MOTORHOME
ROAD TRIP TRAVEL JOURNAL

DATE .... MILEAGE START ....

START TIME .... MILEAGE END ....

ARRIVAL TIME .... MILEAGE TOTAL ....

CAMPSITE NAME ....

ADDRESS 1 ....

ADDRESS 2 ....

POST CODE .... GPS ....

E MAIL .... PHONE ....

WEBSITE WWW...

MY RATING ☆ ☆ ☆ ☆ ☆ NUMBER OF NIGHTS HERE ......

WEATHER .... TEMPERATURE ....

WILDCAMPING LOCATION NOTES

....

....

....

....

.... GPS ....

DAILY COSTS	TODAY'S HIGHLIGHTS
SITE FEES £	....
FUEL £	....
PROPANE £	....
TOLLS £	....
GROCERIES £	....
DINING OUT £	....
ENTERTAINMENT £	....
OTHER COSTS £	....

TO DO TOMORROW

....

....

....

....

NOTES

....

....

....

....

....

....

....

....

SKETCH / KEEPSAKE / PHOTOGRAPH

MOTORHOME
ROAD TRIP TRAVEL JOURNAL

DATE .... MILEAGE START ....

START TIME .... MILEAGE END ....

ARRIVAL TIME .... MILEAGE TOTAL ....

CAMPSITE NAME ....

ADDRESS I ....

ADDRESS 2 ....

POST CODE .... GPS ....

E MAIL .... PHONE ....

WEBSITE WWW...

MY RATING ☆ ☆ ☆ ☆ ☆ NUMBER OF NIGHTS HERE ......

WEATHER .... TEMPERATURE ....

WILDCAMPING LOCATION NOTES

....
....
....
....
.... GPS ....

DAILY COSTS	TODAY'S HIGHLIGHTS
SITE FEES £	....
FUEL £	....
PROPANE £	....
TOLLS £	....
GROCERIES £	....
DINING OUT £	....
ENTERTAINMENT £	....
OTHER COSTS £	....

TO DO TOMORROW

....

....

....

....

NOTES

....

....

....

....

....

....

....

SKETCH / KEEPSAKE / PHOTOGRAPH

MOTORHOME
ROAD TRIP TRAVEL JOURNAL

DATE .... MILEAGE START ....

START TIME .... MILEAGE END ....

ARRIVAL TIME .... MILEAGE TOTAL ....

CAMPSITE NAME ....

ADDRESS 1 ....

ADDRESS 2 ....

POST CODE .... GPS ....

E MAIL .... PHONE ....

WEBSITE WWW..

MY RATING ☆ ☆ ☆ ☆ ☆ NUMBER OF NIGHTS HERE ......

WEATHER .... TEMPERATURE ....

WILDCAMPING LOCATION NOTES

....
....
....
....
.... GPS ....

DAILY COSTS	TODAY'S HIGHLIGHTS
SITE FEES £	....
FUEL £	....
PROPANE £	....
TOLLS £	....
GROCERIES £	....
DINING OUT £	....
ENTERTAINMENT £	....
OTHER COSTS £	....

TO DO TOMORROW

....
....
....
....

NOTES

....

....

....

....

....

....

....

....

SKETCH / KEEPSAKE / PHOTOGRAPH

MOTORHOME
ROAD TRIP TRAVEL JOURNAL

DATE .... MILEAGE START ....

START TIME .... MILEAGE END ....

ARRIVAL TIME .... MILEAGE TOTAL ....

CAMPSITE NAME ....

ADDRESS 1 ....

ADDRESS 2 ....

POST CODE .... GPS ....

E MAIL .... PHONE ....

WEBSITE WWW...

MY RATING ☆ ☆ ☆ ☆ ☆ NUMBER OF NIGHTS HERE ......

WEATHER .... TEMPERATURE ....

WILDCAMPING LOCATION NOTES

....
....
....
....
.... GPS ....

DAILY COSTS		TODAY'S HIGHLIGHTS
SITE FEES	£	....
FUEL	£	....
PROPANE	£	....
TOLLS	£	....
GROCERIES	£	....
DINING OUT	£	....
ENTERTAINMENT	£	....
OTHER COSTS	£	....

TO DO TOMORROW

....

....

....

....

NOTES

....

....

....

....

....

....

....

....

SKETCH / KEEPSAKE / PHOTOGRAPH

MOTORHOME
ROAD TRIP TRAVEL JOURNAL

DATE .... MILEAGE START ....

START TIME .... MILEAGE END ....

ARRIVAL TIME .... MILEAGE TOTAL ....

CAMPSITE NAME ....

ADDRESS 1 ....

ADDRESS 2 ....

POST CODE .... GPS ....

E MAIL .... PHONE ....

WEBSITE WWW..

MY RATING ☆ ☆ ☆ ☆ ☆ NUMBER OF NIGHTS HERE ......

WEATHER .... TEMPERATURE ....

WILDCAMPING LOCATION NOTES

....
....
....
....
.... GPS ....

DAILY COSTS		TODAY'S HIGHLIGHTS
SITE FEES	£	....
FUEL	£	....
PROPANE	£	....
TOLLS	£	....
GROCERIES	£	....
DINING OUT	£	....
ENTERTAINMENT	£	....
OTHER COSTS	£	....

TO DO TOMORROW

....
....
....
....

NOTES

....

....

....

....

....

....

....

SKETCH / KEEPSAKE / PHOTOGRAPH

MOTORHOME
ROAD TRIP TRAVEL JOURNAL

DATE .... MILEAGE START ....

START TIME .... MILEAGE END ....

ARRIVAL TIME .... MILEAGE TOTAL ....

CAMPSITE NAME ....

ADDRESS 1 ....

ADDRESS 2 ....

POST CODE .... GPS ....

E MAIL .... PHONE ....

WEBSITE WWW...

MY RATING ☆ ☆ ☆ ☆ ☆ NUMBER OF NIGHTS HERE ......

WEATHER .... TEMPERATURE ....

WILDCAMPING LOCATION NOTES

....

....

....

.... GPS ....

DAILY COSTS		TODAY'S HIGHLIGHTS
SITE FEES	£	....
FUEL	£	....
PROPANE	£	....
TOLLS	£	....
GROCERIES	£	....
DINING OUT	£	....
ENTERTAINMENT	£	....
OTHER COSTS	£	....

TO DO TOMORROW

....

....

....

....

NOTES

....

....

....

....

....

....

....

....

SKETCH / KEEPSAKE / PHOTOGRAPH

MOTORHOME
ROAD TRIP TRAVEL JOURNAL

DATE .... MILEAGE START ....

START TIME .... MILEAGE END ....

ARRIVAL TIME .... MILEAGE TOTAL ....

CAMPSITE NAME ....

ADDRESS 1 ....

ADDRESS 2 ....

POST CODE .... GPS ....

E MAIL .... PHONE ....

WEBSITE WWW...

MY RATING ☆ ☆ ☆ ☆ ☆ NUMBER OF NIGHTS HERE ......

WEATHER .... TEMPERATURE ....

WILDCAMPING LOCATION NOTES

....
....
....
....
.... GPS ....

DAILY COSTS	TODAY'S HIGHLIGHTS
SITE FEES £	....
FUEL £	....
PROPANE £	....
TOLLS £	....
GROCERIES £	....
DINING OUT £	....
ENTERTAINMENT £	....
OTHER COSTS £	....

TO DO TOMORROW

....

....

....

....

NOTES

....

....

....

....

....

....

....

....

SKETCH / KEEPSAKE / PHOTOGRAPH

MOTORHOME
ROAD TRIP TRAVEL JOURNAL

DATE .... MILEAGE START ....

START TIME .... MILEAGE END ....

ARRIVAL TIME .... MILEAGE TOTAL ....

CAMPSITE NAME ....

ADDRESS 1 ....

ADDRESS 2 ....

POST CODE .... GPS ....

E MAIL .... PHONE ....

WEBSITE WWW...

MY RATING ☆ ☆ ☆ ☆ ☆ NUMBER OF NIGHTS HERE ......

WEATHER .... TEMPERATURE ....

WILDCAMPING LOCATION NOTES

....
....
....
....
.... GPS ....

DAILY COSTS	TODAY'S HIGHLIGHTS
SITE FEES £	....
FUEL £	....
PROPANE £	....
TOLLS £	....
GROCERIES £	....
DINING OUT £	....
ENTERTAINMENT £	....
OTHER COSTS £	....

TO DO TOMORROW

....
....
....
....

NOTES

....

....

....

....

....

....

....

SKETCH / KEEPSAKE / PHOTOGRAPH

MOTORHOME
ROAD TRIP TRAVEL JOURNAL

DATE .... MILEAGE START ....

START TIME .... MILEAGE END ....

ARRIVAL TIME .... MILEAGE TOTAL ....

CAMPSITE NAME ....

ADDRESS 1 ....

ADDRESS 2 ....

POST CODE .... GPS ....

E MAIL .... PHONE ....

WEBSITE WWW..

MY RATING ☆ ☆ ☆ ☆ ☆ NUMBER OF NIGHTS HERE ......

WEATHER .... TEMPERATURE ....

WILDCAMPING LOCATION NOTES

....
....
....
....
.... GPS ....

DAILY COSTS

SITE FEES	£ ....
FUEL	£ ....
PROPANE	£ ....
TOLLS	£ ....
GROCERIES	£ ....
DINING OUT	£ ....
ENTERTAINMENT	£ ....
OTHER COSTS	£ ....

TODAY'S HIGHLIGHTS

....
....
....
....
....
....
....

TO DO TOMORROW

....

....

....

....

NOTES

....

....

....

....

....

....

....

....

SKETCH / KEEPSAKE / PHOTOGRAPH

MOTORHOME
ROAD TRIP TRAVEL JOURNAL

DATE .... MILEAGE START ....

START TIME .... MILEAGE END ....

ARRIVAL TIME .... MILEAGE TOTAL ....

CAMPSITE NAME ....

ADDRESS I ....

ADDRESS 2 ....

POST CODE .... GPS ....

E MAIL .... PHONE ....

WEBSITE WWW.......................................

MY RATING ☆ ☆ ☆ ☆ ☆ NUMBER OF NIGHTS HERE ......

WEATHER .... TEMPERATURE ....

WILDCAMPING LOCATION NOTES

....
....
....
....
.... GPS ....

DAILY COSTS

TODAY'S HIGHLIGHTS

SITE FEES £ ....

FUEL £ ....

PROPANE £ ....

TOLLS £ ....

GROCERIES £ ....

DINING OUT £ ....

ENTERTAINMENT £ ....

OTHER COSTS £ ....

TO DO TOMORROW

....
....
....
....

NOTES

....

....

....

....

....

....

....

....

SKETCH / KEEPSAKE / PHOTOGRAPH

MOTORHOME
ROAD TRIP TRAVEL JOURNAL

DATE .... MILEAGE START ....

START TIME .... MILEAGE END ....

ARRIVAL TIME .... MILEAGE TOTAL ....

CAMPSITE NAME ....

ADDRESS 1 ....

ADDRESS 2 ....

POST CODE .... GPS ....

E MAIL .... PHONE ....

WEBSITE WWW..

MY RATING ☆ ☆ ☆ ☆ ☆ NUMBER OF NIGHTS HERE ......

WEATHER .... TEMPERATURE ....

WILDCAMPING LOCATION NOTES

....

....

....

....

.... GPS ....

DAILY COSTS	TODAY'S HIGHLIGHTS
SITE FEES £	....
FUEL £	....
PROPANE £	....
TOLLS £	....
GROCERIES £	....
DINING OUT £	....
ENTERTAINMENT £	....
OTHER COSTS £	....

TO DO TOMORROW

....

....

....

....

NOTES

....

....

....

....

....

....

....

....

SKETCH / KEEPSAKE / PHOTOGRAPH

MOTORHOME
ROAD TRIP TRAVEL JOURNAL

DATE .... MILEAGE START ....

START TIME .... MILEAGE END ....

ARRIVAL TIME .... MILEAGE TOTAL ....

CAMPSITE NAME ....

ADDRESS 1 ....

ADDRESS 2 ....

POST CODE .... GPS ....

E MAIL .... PHONE ....

WEBSITE WWW..

MY RATING ☆ ☆ ☆ ☆ ☆ NUMBER OF NIGHTS HERE ......

WEATHER .... TEMPERATURE ....

WILDCAMPING LOCATION NOTES

....
....
....
.... GPS ....

DAILY COSTS		TODAY'S HIGHLIGHTS
SITE FEES	£	....
FUEL	£	....
PROPANE	£	....
TOLLS	£	....
GROCERIES	£	....
DINING OUT	£	....
ENTERTAINMENT	£	....
OTHER COSTS	£	....

TO DO TOMORROW

....
....
....
....

NOTES

....

....

....

....

....

....

....

....

SKETCH / KEEPSAKE / PHOTOGRAPH

MOTORHOME
ROAD TRIP TRAVEL JOURNAL

DATE .... MILEAGE START ....

START TIME .... MILEAGE END ....

ARRIVAL TIME .... MILEAGE TOTAL ....

CAMPSITE NAME ....

ADDRESS 1 ....

ADDRESS 2 ....

POST CODE .... GPS ....

E MAIL .... PHONE ....

WEBSITE WWW...

MY RATING ☆ ☆ ☆ ☆ ☆ NUMBER OF NIGHTS HERE ......

WEATHER .... TEMPERATURE ....

WILDCAMPING LOCATION NOTES

....

....

....

....

.... GPS ....

DAILY COSTS	TODAY'S HIGHLIGHTS
SITE FEES £	....
FUEL £	....
PROPANE £	....
TOLLS £	....
GROCERIES £	....
DINING OUT £	....
ENTERTAINMENT £	....
OTHER COSTS £	....

TO DO TOMORROW

....

....

....

....

NOTES

....

....

....

....

....

....

....

SKETCH / KEEPSAKE / PHOTOGRAPH

Printed in Great Britain
by Amazon